35 Ea ,

Tray Bakes,

Slices &

Bar Cookie

Recipes

-

Thirty-Five

Tried and Tested Recipes

Elizabeth Daniel

Copyright Notice

INTRODUCTION

Why A Cookbook On Traybakes & Slices?

This book began as something of a personal baking adventure.

When my children began to leave home and with no ravenous mouths to feed, I wanted to express my love of baking, but without affecting my own waistline!

So, I began sharing my baking. It started simply enough, sharing cakes at work, at church, even with a local charity.

Eager to experiment and branch out, I began searching out and adapting traybake recipes, keen to find some recipes that people would enjoy eating.

"35 Easy Tray Bakes, Slices & Bar Cooking Recipes" is the result of two years of testing and tasting.

I'd like to say a huge thank you for all those who have so willingly tested the results, this book wouldn't be here without you.

I hope that you have as much fun trying out these recipes as I did putting them together.

Happy baking!

Elizabeth

Introduction to this Cookbook

Tray bakes, slices and bar cookies are tasty, delicious and easy-to-make treats that everyone will enjoy.

Did you know that what's known as a *bar cookie* in the US, is called a *tray bake* in the UK and in Australia it's a *slice*?

Each country has their own most popular and well-loved recipes and we'll be sharing these as well as several of our own favourites in this book.

Enjoy making these crowd-pleasing recipes that everyone will love. Whether you're looking for something that's simple to bake, are unsure of baking or perhaps you just want to try something new and a little different.

Just remember to grease or line your baking tray, check your oven is reliable, you can be confident of turning out great cakes time and time again.

Tray bakes are perfect for office, birthday parties, family gatherings, potluck dinner, fund raising, charity stalls, after-school snacks, bazaars, church socials, fetes, Christmas fairs, cake sales and after school snacks. For families, it's a great way to bake a generous amount of cake on a budget.

So, exactly what is a traybake, bar cookie, sheet cake or slice recipe?

It's usually a cake or slice cooked in an oblong shaped tray, rather than the traditional deep or round cake tin, catering for 10 or more slices. Bar cookies are cookies that the dough or batter is poured or pressed into a pan, then cut into bars after baking.

This is a great way to bake your favourite cakes in one big batch, then freeze them to enjoy throughout the week. They're so convenient, and save money by baking all you need in one batch.

Each recipe offers two sets of ingredients, with batch sizes to bake for 12-18, and a second list of ingredients for up to 24 or 36 servings. So you should be able to find the perfect recipe for any size of gathering. Cut into bite-size pieces for a festive treat, or into generous slices for your fund raising event, it's up to you.

All you need to know are a few handy recipes and you're ready to go. For those on special diets, we've included several recipes suitable for those with special dietary needs (e.g. gluten free, dairy free, etc).

We've included some classic favourites, such as lemon drizzle and chocolate brownies. There's also a chapter of no-bake, no-cook recipes which you can put together with the help of a microwave or stove top.

The only challenge is that your cakes will taste so good that you may find them hard to resist!

Happy making and baking!

Your Questions Answered

Sometimes it's hard to know which recipe to try first, so here's a few of your questions answered, which will help you decide!

Which cake is best served warm?

The Blueberry and Lemon Cake really does melt in your mouth whilst it's still warm.   The Almond Frangipane also tastes delicious fresh from the oven.

What recipes can I make ahead of time?

The flavour of some cakes improves with time, try the French Almond Cake or the Chocolate Brownies, which keep well.   Banana Bread also has a richer, deeper flavour if made a couple days before it's eaten. You can also make and freeze the Malty Indulgence tray bake, for up to 14 days.

My kids don't love fruit or vegetables, but they love cake, what can I bake them to encourage them to eat more healthily?

Two favourites are Dorset Apple Cake and Carrot Cake. Banana Bread uses bananas, honey and pecans as ingredients. Hawaiian Cake is full of delicious pineapple and quite irresistible.

Are there any recipes that are no-bake recipes?

Yes, we have a whole section! Our family favourite is the Chocolate Tray Bake/Polish Cake.

Are there any recipes suitable for a diabetic?

We suggest choosing recipes that are low in carb and sugar per slice, so a thin slice of the Carpathian Mountain Cake (Karpatka), or the freezer friendly Chocolate Brownie.

Any ideas what I can make for a kids party?

The Jelly Slice is colourful and eye-catching, so great for kids. Chocolate cake or brownies is great for parties, but something new to try could be Blondies, which are deliciously chewy and moist.

I'd like something different for a special occasion, what would you suggest?

For something different, try making a tray of Lamington bake, they look lovely and disappear quickly.

What about brownies that turn out every time, mine never seem to turn out right?

I know just how you feel! You'll find several recipes for brownies to suit every taste, a good one to try first is our Molten Chocolate Brownies.

I'd like to bake something simple for Christmas, what do you suggest?

A distinctly festive cake, is Cranberry Cake, flavoured with oranges and bursting with rich cranberries.

How about making a batch of brownies, for any unexpected guests?

Almond Frangipane is a treat for any occasion.

I need a recipe for a gluten-free cake, what can I bake?

The All-in-One Chocolate Cake is a great cake for anyone who is gluten intolerant, and it tastes very chocolatey.

The French Almond Cake is also a family favourite, and can be made as a gluten free bake.

If you're happy to experiment, for recipes where flour is the only ingredient containing gluten, try substituting with gluten-free buckwheat flour.

Why not try the Moist Chocolate Cake, made with almonds and grated beetroot, which is full of chocolatey flavour.

What's the easiest recipe to bake from my store cupboard?

Of course, it will depend what you've got in your store cupboard. Perhaps the Sweet Cornbread, Bread Pudding (to use up leftover bread) or the Blondies.

Do you have any dairy-free recipes?

Yes, try the All-in-One Chocolate Cake. It's easy and delicious and we reckon no-one will guess it's dairy free!

Another option is the Hawaiian Cake, full of fruity goodness.

Cooks Tips

Cooking terminology varies from country to country. What is known in the UK as a baking tray or tin is known as a Lamington pan in Australia and a jelly roll pan in the USA. *We will endeavour to use the term pan or tin throughout this book.*

For *chilled slice* recipes such as the Mars Bar or Hedgehog slice, use a hot knife (dip blade in a mug of hot water) to cut into pieces before fully cooled.

No-bake recipes will usually keep well in an air-tight container for three or four days, if you can resist them that long!

Please Read Before Baking!

Here's a few things you'll need to know about these recipes.

Salt - few of the recipes use added salt. This is deliberate, as we are a salt-free household. You may choose to add salt to suit your tastebuds.

Butter - We only use unsalted butter in these recipes. If you are used to salt in your baking, you'll need to add salt to taste.

Sugar - unless specified, where the recipe says 'sugar', all the recipes have been tested using caster sugar. We have reduced the sugar content in most recipes. If you have a sweet tooth, feel free to add a little extra!

Milk - we tested most of these recipes using either dairy milk or soya milk, both worked well.

Flour - If you only have plain flour, you can use 225g flour and 2 ½ level tsp baking powder to *replace self-raising flour.*

Baking Tray/Tin/Pan Size - for the smaller size recipes serving 12-14 we used a pan size 23cm x 23cm (9" x 9"). For larger recipes we used trays measuring approximately 37cm x 27cm (14.5" x 11"). Pans are typically around 3-4cm deep.

Always grease or line your baking tray to ensure that you can cut, slice and remove your cake with ease.

Portion sizes - most of our portions are small, just a bite size amount for each person. Please note that if you're baking for a bake sale, you may want to increase the portion sizes from those suggested.

Oven temperatures - all temperatures in our recipes assume a conventional oven temperature. If *you have a fan oven*, reduce the temperature accordingly
(e.g. for 180°C conventional, use 170°C fan oven).

Let's get baking!

TABLE OF CONTENTS

Why A Cookbook on Traybakes & Slices? _____ 2

Introduction to this Cookbook _____ ??

Your Questions Answered _____ 6

Cooks Tips _____ 10

Table of Contents _____ 14

QUICK & EASY FAVOURITES _____ 17

Orange & Poppyseed Cake _____ 18

French Far Breton(Far Aux Pruneaux) _____ 20

Carrot Cake Tray Bake _____ 22

Lemon Drizzle Tray Bake / Orange Cake ___ 24

Sweet Cornbread Tray Bake _____ 26

Gingerbread Tray Bake _____ 28

French Almond Cake Recipe _____ 30

CHOCOLATE TEMPTATIONS _____ 33

Chocolate Chip Slice _____ 34

Molten Chocolate Brownies _____ 36

Caramel Slice _____ 38

Banoffee Cake _____ 40

Blondies _____ 42

Mississippi Mud Cake | Marshmallow Brownies 44

FRUITY GOODNESS 47

- Dorset Apple Cake Slice 48
- Cranberry Cake 50
- Hawaiian Tray Bake Cake / Slice 52
- Raspberry Yoghurt Cake 54
- Blueberry & Lemon Cake 56
- Banana Bread Tray Bake 58
- Raspberry & Coconut Slice 60

FUN FOR KIDS 63

- Chocolate Toffee Slice 64
- Apricot Muesli Bar | Muesli Slice 66
- Jelly Slice 68
- Bread Pudding Slice 70

GLUTEN FREE 73

- Chocolate Brownie Tray Bake 74
- Flapjack Traybake 76
- All-in-One Chocolate Cake 78
- Gluten Free Brownies Tray Bake 80

NO BAKE / NO COOK _____ 83

    Polish Cake | Chocolate Tiffin Slice _____ 84

    Hedgehog Slice _____ 86

    Malty Indulgence Tray Bake _____ 88

BAKE TO IMPRESS _____ 91

    Ginger Butter Cake _____ 92

    Lamington Bake _____ 94

    Chocolate Treacle Brownie Slice _____ 96

    Carpathian Mountain Cake (Karpatka) _____ 98

    Almond Frangipane _____ 100

QUICK & EASY FAVOURITES

Orange & Poppyseed Cake

Poppy seed adds a distinctive taste and texture to this deliciously different cake.

Ingredients

Serves 24-32

450g butter
4 oranges
8 eggs
300g caster sugar
2 tsp vanilla extract
550g self raising flour
4 tsp baking powder
6 tbsp poppy seeds

Serves 12-16

225g butter
2 oranges
4 eggs
150g caster sugar
1 tsp vanilla extract
275g self raising flour
2tsp baking powder
3 tbsp poppy seeds

Preheat oven to 175C, 350F

Melt butter

Liquidise or blend whole oranges with melted butter

Transfer to a mixing bowl

Add eggs, sugar and vanilla and mix together

Add flour, baking powder and poppy seeds & stir well

Bake in a greased pan for 35-40 minutes, or until a skewer comes out clean

Cooks Note: You'll need a liquidiser or a stick/hand blender for this recipe.

French Far Breton
(Far Aux Pruneaux)

A delicious custardy dessert or cake, traditionally made in the Brittany area in northern France.

Ingredients

Serves 18-20

150g prunes, halved and de-stoned
60g raisins (optional)
1 teabag
200g plain flour
150g sugar
4 large eggs (or 6 small)
600ml milk
50g butter
1 tsp vanilla extract
icing sugar (optional)

Serves 6-10

75g prunes, halved and de-stoned
30g raisins (optional)
1 teabag
100g plain flour
75g sugar
2 large eggs (or 3 small)
300ml milk
25g butter
½ tsp vanilla extract
icing sugar (optional)

Preheat oven to 375C, 190F, GM5

Soak prunes and raisins in 250ml tea (made with teabag) for at least 1 hour, or overnight

Mix together flour, sugar and eggs

Slowly add milk and vanilla, stirring well

Melt butter and stir in to mix

Pour batter into a well greased baking tin

Drop in the drained fruit, as evenly as possible

Bake in oven for 40-60 minutes, until set

Set aside and leave to cool

Cut into slices and serve dusted with icing sugar

Cooks Note: Use Earl Grey, Lady Grey or your favourite teabags for a slightly different twist in flavour.

For a dairy-free Far Breton, use unsweetened soya milk and omit butter.

French Far Breton

Carrot Cake Tray Bake

This is always popular and everyone seems to have their own recipe, this is my favourite.

Ingredients

Serves 35

Cake
1 teabag
200g raisins or sultanas
350g butter
350g soft brown sugar
6 eggs
500g self raising flour
1tsp vanilla extract
Grated rind of 1 orange
700g roughly grated carrots
Juice of 1 orange (less 2 tbsp for topping)

Topping
500g cream cheese
4 tbsp icing sugar
2 tbsp orange juice

Serves 18

Cake
1 teabag
100g raisins or sultanas
175g butter
175g soft brown sugar
3 eggs
250g self raising flour
½ tsp vanilla extract
½ grated rind of 1 orange
350g roughly grated carrots
Juice of ½ orange (less 1 tbsp)

Topping
250g cream cheese
2 tbsp icing sugar
1 tbsp orange juice

Preheat oven for 180C, 350F, GM4

Add teabag to ½ pint of boiling water to make tea

Cover the raisins or sultanas with hot tea and leave to soak for at least 15 minutes

Mix the butter, sugar together until smooth

Add in the eggs and flour and mix until smooth

Add the vanilla extract, drained fruit, grated rind of orange and mix

Add in the grated carrots and mix together - you may need to mix this by hand

Spoon evenly into baking pan and bake for 45-55 minutes

Check that it is cooked by inserting a knife or skewer in until it comes out again clean

Retaining 2 tbsp for the topping, drizzle the orange juice across the top of the cake

Leave to cool

Mix all the topping ingredients together

Once cooled, use a flat knife or spatula to spread the topping evenly across the top of the cake

Cut into 35 squares

This recipe makes a cake which is dense, yet moist and crumbly. For a lighter cake, use only 500g/250g grated carrots.

Cooks Note: You can freeze the cake without the topping, then defrost and add topping.

Lemon Drizzle Tray Bake | Orange Cake

This is an easy tray bake and simply delicious. This is my 'go-to' recipe whenever I need to bake in a hurry and, best of all, everyone seems to love eating it.

Ingredients

Serves 24-36

Cake

350g butter
350g sugar
6 eggs
450g self raising flour
3 tsp baking powder
grated rind of 3 lemons/oranges
6 tbsp milk

Topping

Juice of 3 lemons/oranges
125g caster sugar

Serves 12-18

Cake

175g butter
175g sugar
3 eggs
225g self raising flour
$1\frac{1}{2}$ tsp baking powder
grated rind of $1\frac{1}{2}$ lemons/oranges
3 tbsp milk

Topping

Juice of $1\frac{1}{2}$ lemons/oranges
65g caster sugar

Preheat oven to 350F, 180F, GM4

Mix together the butter and sugar

Add the eggs, self raising flour, baking powder and lemon/orange rind

Mix together, adding the milk, to form a dropping consistency

Beat well, until light and airy

Pour into a greased or lined pan

Bake in oven for 30-40 minutes

While cake is still hot, mix topping ingredients into a paste and spoon over top of cake

Use back of spoon to spread across the top and into the corners

Leave to cool

Sweet Cornbread Tray Bake

First tried warm from the oven in a kitchen in West Africa and never forgotten. This sweet cornbread is best served fresh and warm.

Ingredients

Serves 24-40

300g plain flour
2 ½ tbsp baking powder
225g sugar
1 tsp salt
150g butter, softened
325g yellow cornmeal/polenta
4 eggs, beaten
500ml milk *or* buttermilk

Serves 12-20

150g plain flour
4 tsp baking powder
110g sugar
3/4 tsp salt
75g butter, softened
160g yellow cornmeal/polenta
2 eggs, beaten
250ml milk *or* buttermilk

Preheat oven to 195C, 400F, GM6

Grease a baking tin

Sift flour and baking powder into a bowl

Add sugar, salt and butter

Beat until butter is size of breadcrumbs

Stir in cornmeal

Add eggs and milk

Mix together until smooth to create a batter

Pour into prepared pan

Bake for 20-25 minutes or until it turns to a golden brown

Gingerbread Tray Bake

This is a classic and timeless recipe, with a wonderfully rich flavour, handed down by my aunt. Gingerbread is supposed to keep well, though it's so more-ish that we've never yet found out if this is true.

Ingredients

Makes 30-35

300g butter
250g demerara sugar
1 heaped tbsp marmalade
300g treacle
425ml milk
250g self raising flour
300g wholemeal flour
2 tsp ground ginger
2 tsp mixed spice
5 eggs (beaten)
2 tsp baking powder
1 tsp bicarbonate of soda
pinch of salt

Makes 14-16

150g butter
125g demerara sugar
½ tbsp marmalade
150g treacle
200ml milk
125g self raising flour
150g wholemeal flour
1 tsp ground ginger
1 tsp mixed spice
3 eggs (beaten)
1 tsp baking powder
½ tsp bicarb of soda
pinch of salt

Preheat oven to 170C, 325F, GM3

Melt the butter

Add sugar, marmalade, treacle and milk to butter

Sift flours and spices into a bowl

Add eggs, baking powder & bicarb of soda, to the flour and spices

Add sugar mixture

Beat together until smooth

Pour into a greased or lined tin

Bake in oven for 30-40 minutes

Cooks Note: If you like, top with icing. Mix 300g icing sugar with enough water to give a soft consistency Spread over the top of the cake and leave to set.

Tastes fabulous served warm, enjoy with a dollop of ice cream.

You can use dark brown sugar instead of demerara
You can replace the wholemeal flour with buckwheat flour, for a gluten free version.

French Almond Cake

The French certainly know a thing or two when it comes to baking, and their almond cake is no exception. The secret to this recipe is using real butter, which gives it a deep, satisfying flavour.

Ingredients

Serves 24

250g softened butter
250g caster sugar
5 eggs
200g ground almonds/almond flour
100g flour
3 tsp baking powder
2 tsp vanilla extract or vanilla bean paste
2 tbsp milk
Sprinkle of flaked almonds (optional)

Serves 12

125g softened butter
130g caster sugar
3 eggs
100g ground almonds/almond flour
50g flour
1 ½ tsp baking powder
1 tsp vanilla extract or vanilla bean paste
1 tbsp milk
Sprinkle of flaked almonds (optional)

Preheat oven to 180C, 350F, GM4

Beat together butter and sugar until creamy

One at a time, add the eggs, mixing well after each addition

Add the almonds, flour, baking powder, vanilla and milk

Spoon into greased baking tin

Sprinkle over flaked almonds

Bake in oven for 35-45 minutes

Cooks Note: The flavour of this cake improves further, if left for 24 hours. Before serving, dust top with icing sugar.

CHOCOLATE TEMPTATIONS

Chocolate Chip Slice

A great store cupboard recipe - quick and easy to make with just enough chocolate to keep everyone happy.

Ingredients

Makes 24-32

350g butter
675g self raising flour
3 tsp baking powder
250g light brown soft sugar
200g chocolate chips
6 eggs (beaten)
250ml milk (to mix)

Makes 12-16

175g butter
325g self raising flour
1 ½ tsp baking powder
125g light brown soft sugar
100g chocolate chips
3 eggs (beaten)
100ml milk (to mix)

Preheat oven to 180C, 350F, GM4

Grease baking tin

Rub butter into flour and baking powder

Add in sugar and chocolate chips

Mix in beaten eggs and milk

Spoon into baking tin and smooth

Cooks Note: If you don't have any chocolate chips, cut a chocolate
bar into small chunks

Bake for 35-40 minutes

Remove from oven and set aside to cool

Slice and serve

* This recipe freezes well

Molten Chocolate Brownies

After struggling for years to find the perfect brownie recipe, my journey for chocolatey perfection is finally over. These are naughty, indulgent and simply delicious.

Ingredients

Serves 16-24

400g dark chocolate (preferably 70%)
1 tbsp hazelnut chocolate spread - optional
180g butter
175g caster sugar
6 eggs
50g ground almonds /almond flour (4 tbsp)

Serves 10-12

200g dark chocolate (preferably 70%)
½ tbsp hazelnut chocolate spread - optional
90g butter
90g caster sugar
3 eggs
25g ground almonds /almond flour (2 tbsp)

Preheat oven to 175C, 325F, GM3

In a bowl over hot water, melt the chocolate

Once melted, stir in the hazelnut spread

Beat butter and sugar together

Separate the eggs

Slowly mix in egg yolks

Now stir in ground almonds

In a separate bowl whisk the egg whites until soft peaks form

Pour molten chocolate into the butter and eggs mixture

Stir together

Finally, add in the egg whites, stirring gently with a metal spoon until all egg white is mixed in with no white specks visible

Pour into greased baking tin

Bake in oven for 18 minutes

Turn oven off and leave for 5 minutes

Remove from oven to cool

Cooks Note: These brownies are best made ahead of time, as they taste best once fully cooled. Serve chilled, straight from the fridge.

Caramel Slice

Loved everywhere, this is also known as Millionaire Shortbread, Tiffin, Wellington Squares (or triangles), Caramel Shortbread or Caramel Shortcake.

When you taste the finished result, you'll discover that your efforts were not in vain.

Makes 12-16 (regular squares)
or 25 (mini bite-size squares)

Ingredients

Shortbread Base

200g shortbread biscuits, crushed
50g butter

Caramel Filling

397g tin condensed milk
150g butter
125g dark brown soft sugar

Chocolate Topping

200g milk chocolate

Shortbread Base

Grease base of pan with a knob of butter

Melt butter

Stir in shortbread biscuits

Mix well

Press gently into the base

Chill

Caramel Filling

In a saucepan mix the condensed milk, butter and sugar

Over a low heat, stir gently until first bubbles come to the surface

Turn off heat

Pour over biscuit base

Chill

Chocolate Topping

In a microwave, or bowl over a pan of hot water, melt chocolate

Pour over top of caramel and smooth out evenly

Set aside to cool

When almost set, cut into slices

Refrigerate

Cooks Note: If you leave this in the fridge, the chocolate may crack when you come to cut it, so it's best to cut into slices before refrigerating.

Banoffee Cake

A delicious recipe dreamt up by my lovely daughter-in-law. This mixture of banana and toffee flavours will have you and your guests coming back for more.

Ingredients

Serves 24-32

150g butter
350g light brown sugar
350g flour
4 tsp baking powder
2 tsp bicarbonate of soda
4 eggs
6 mashed bananas (approx 600g)
200g caramel chocolates (we used Cadbury Caramel Nibbles)

Serves 12-16

75g butter
175g light brown sugar
175g flour
2 tsp baking powder
1 tsp bicarbonate of soda
2 eggs
3 mashed bananas (approx 300g)
100g caramel chocolates (we used Cadbury Caramel Nibbles)

Preheat oven to 170C, 325F, GM3

Beat butter and sugar until soft

Add flour, baking powder, bicarbonate of soda and eggs.

Stir in mashed banana

Stir in caramel chocolates by hand

Pour into a greased pan

Bake for 30-35 minutes (or until a knife or skewer inserted near the centre comes out clean)

Cooks Note: We also tested this recipe with chopped caramel chocolate eggs, and it tasted great. Feel free to experiment.

Blondies

This is a chewy, moist version of a brownie, but without the cocoa, and certainly is a traybake that disappears very fast in our household!

Ingredients

Serves 20-24

175g butter
270g dark brown sugar
300g flour (plain or all-purpose)
2 eggs
2 tsp vanilla extract or ½ tsp vanilla bean paste
1 tsp baking powder
½ tsp bicarb of soda (baking soda)
100g white or dark chocolate chips or fudge chunks

Serves 10-12

85g butter
135g dark brown sugar
150g flour (plain or all-purpose)
1 egg
1 tsp vanilla extract or 1/4 tsp vanilla bean paste
½ tsp baking powder
1/4 tsp bicarb of soda (baking soda)
50g white or dark chocolate chips or fudge chunks

Preheat oven to 180C, 350F, GM4

Melt butter and mix together with sugar

Beat and stir in egg, whisking together

Add flour, vanilla, baking powder and bicarb of soda

Mix well

Add chocolate chips and fold in

Pour into well-greased tin

Bake for 18-25 minutes until just cooked

When cool, cut into small bite-size pieces

Cooks Note: Instead of store-bought chocolate chips, try chopping a chocolate bar into small pieces.

Mississippi Mud Cake *or* Marshmallow Brownies

A chocolate cake with a fudge-like topping and filled with soft marshmallows, worth getting sticky fingers for!

Ingredients

Serves 30

Cake	*Icing*
500g butter	60g butter
450g plain flour	3 tbsp milk
120g cocoa powder	1 ½ tbsp cocoa
610g sugar	135g icing (powdered) sugar
100g pecans (chopped)	
8 large eggs	
2 tsp vanilla extract	
150g mini-marshmallows	

Serves 15

Cake	*Icing*
250g butter	30g butter
225g plain flour	1 ½ tbsp milk
60g cocoa powder	3/4 tbsp cocoa
295g sugar	65g icing (powdered) sugar
50g pecans (chopped)	
4 large eggs	
1 tsp vanilla extract	
75g mini-marshmallows	

Cake

Preheat oven to 180C, 350F, GM4

Melt butter gently in a pan or microwave

Set aside to cool slightly

Sieve flour and cocoa into a bowl

Add sugar, and pecans

Stir in eggs and vanilla

Stir in marshmallows and melted butter

Pour the mixture into a greased baking tin

Bake for 25-30 minutes in oven

Topping

Ten minutes before the cake is ready to remove from the oven, prepare the topping

Melt the butter

Stir in milk

Sieve the cocoa powder and icing/confectioners sugar into a separate bowl

Add in the butter and milk mix, stirring until smooth

Remove cake from oven and quickly pour the topping over the hot cake

Return to the oven for 3-4 minutes

Remove from oven and set aside to cool

Cooks Note: The pecans in this recipe are optional. If you don't have mini-marshmallows, use a sharp knife to cut regular marshmallows into small pieces.

FRUITY GOODNESS

Dorset Apple Cake Slice

After enjoying some delicious Dorset Apple Cake from Dorset bakeries, here's my own take on this wonderfully moist and spicy cake.

Ingredients

Make 35 pieces

800g cooking apples
1 lemon
400g butter (softened)
500g caster sugar
600g self raising flour
4 tsp baking powder
1 tsp mixed spice
1 tsp ground nutmeg
7 eggs
3 tsp vanilla extract
2 tbsp milk (or to mix)
sugar to sprinkle

Makes 16 pieces

450g cooking apples
½ lemon
230g butter (softened)
250g caster sugar
350g self raising flour
2 tsp baking powder
½ tsp mixed spice
½ tsp ground nutmeg
4 eggs
2 tsp vanilla extract
1 tbsp milk (or to mix)
sugar to sprinkle

Preheat oven to 180C, 350F, GM4

Peel and core cooking apples

Cut peeled and cored apples into small pieces

Grate lemon zest

Squeeze lemon juice into a bowl

Mix apple pieces in lemon juice (to prevent browning)

Cream butter, sugar and lemon zest together until light

Sieve the flour, baking powder and spices into a bowl

Add in eggs, a little at a time, adding a spoonful of flour mix with each addition

Add the remaining flour mix and vanilla

Add milk until the mixture is of a dropping consistency

Drain the lemon juice from the apple pieces

Add apple and mix well

Spoon the mixture into a greased or lined baking tin

Sprinkle top lightly with sugar

Bake for 45-55 minutes until golden

Cool

Slice into pieces

Enjoy warm with a spoonful of crème fraîche or cold with a cup of tea

Cooks Note: If you don't have mixed spice, replace with ground cinnamon.

Cranberry Cake

This is a lovely cake that allows you to enjoy the flavour of cranberries at any time of year, not just at Christmas and Thanksgiving. It's also the perfect pick-me-up cake for cold winter days.

Ingredients

Serves 20-24

300g cranberries (fresh or frozen)
375g flour
1 generous pinch salt
2 tsp vanilla
½ grated rind of orange (optional)
5 eggs
600g sugar
175g butter
3 tbsp milk

Serves 10-12

150g cranberries (fresh or frozen)
180g flour
1 pinch salt
1 tsp vanilla
1/4 grated rind of orange (optional)
3 eggs
320g sugar
90g butter
1 ½ tbsp milk

Preheat oven to 140C, 275F, GM1

Spread out cranberries on a baking tin and place in oven for 2-4 minutes

Meanwhile, place flour and salt in a large bowl

Remove cranberries from oven and spoon cranberries and their juice into flour

With a spoon or fork, gently toss cranberries in flour

Add vanilla and orange rind

Set aside cranberry mix

Increase heat in oven to 170C, 325F, GM3

Line baking tin with baking parchment

Beat eggs and sugar together with an electric beater for 5-8 minutes until almost white and silky smooth

Add butter and beat for a further 2 minutes

Beat in the milk

Fold in the flour and cranberry mix

Pour batter into greased baking tin

Bake for 20-25 minutes, until top is just lightly golden

Turn oven off and leave cake in oven for 5 minutes

Remove form oven and leave to cool

Cooks Note: Lightly roasting the cranberries before baking really brings out their sweetness.

Hawaiian Tray Bake Cake / Slice

If you like carrot cake, you may love this slice recipe which is particularly popular 'down under' in Australia.

Ingredients

Serves 24-32

450g self raising flour
2 tsp baking powder
2 tsp cinnamon
200g soft brown sugar
60g desiccated coconut
4 eggs
375ml oil (or melted butter *not dairy free)
Juice and zest of two oranges/lemons
4 ripe bananas (approx. 420g)
2 * 450g cans (600g drained weight) pineapple pieces

Serves 12-16

225g self raising flour
1 tsp baking powder
1 tsp cinnamon
100g soft brown sugar
30g desiccated coconut
2 eggs
190ml oil (or melted butter *not dairy free)
Juice and zest of one orange/lemon
2 ripe bananas (approx. 210g)
450g can (300g drained weight) pineapple pieces

Preheat oven to 180C, 350F, GM4

Drain pineapple juice from can

Sieve flour, baking powder and cinnamon into a bowl

Stir in sugar, coconut, eggs, oil/butter, orange/lemon zest and juice

Mash banana and stir into mix

With a spoon, stir in pineapple pieces

Pour into a greased or lined baking tin

Bake for 40-45 minutes

Leave to cool in pan

Cooks Note: Crushed pineapple or chopped pineapple rings can be used instead of pineapple pieces.

Dairy free recipe

Raspberry Yoghurt Cake

This is an easy to put together cake, based on a delicious French recipe.

Ingredients

Serves 24-30

500ml plain yoghurt
190ml oil
6 eggs
270g brown sugar
2 tsp vanilla extract or vanilla bean paste
450g plain flour
4 tsp baking powder
1 tsp baking soda
55g ground almonds
375g raspberries
100g flour

Serves 12-15

250ml plain yoghurt
95ml oil
3 eggs
135g brown sugar
1 tsp vanilla extract or vanilla bean paste
220g plain flour
2 tsp baking powder
½ tsp baking soda
25g ground almonds
175g raspberries
50g flour

Preheat oven to 180C, 350F, GM4

Line or grease baking tin

In a bowl together yoghurt, oil, eggs, sugar and vanilla

In a separate bowl, sift flower, baking powder and baking soda together

Stir in ground almonds

Add dried ingredients into yoghurt mix and stir together until smooth

In a bowl, place 50g flour and mix raspberries in ensuring that they are coated with flour

Remove raspberries from flour mix and retain

Pour two-thirds of the batter into baking tin

Top with raspberries, then cover with remaining batter

Bake for 35-45 minutes, until golden brown

Leave to cool and cut into slices

Cooks Note: You may use whatever fresh or frozen (no need to defrost) berries you have available - e.g. blueberries, cherries, blackcurrants, blackberries, etc

We made this cake with frozen raspberries, bought in season and frozen, great if you want to enjoy a real taste of summer at any time of year.

Add a pinch of salt with the ground almonds for a better flavour.

Blueberry & Lemon Cake

This cake is bursting with blueberry goodness and is simply delicious when eaten warm.

Ingredients

Serves 24-32

160g butter
200g caster sugar
zest of 1 lemon
4 eggs
2 tsp vanilla
500g flour
4 tsp baking powder
350g blueberries (fresh or frozen)
350ml buttermilk
juice of 1 lemon
2 Tbsp sugar

Serves 12-16

80g butter
100g caster sugar
zest of ½ lemon
2 eggs
1 tsp vanilla
250g flour
2 tsp baking powder
200g blueberries (fresh or frozen)
175ml buttermilk
juice of ½lemon
1 Tbsp sugar

Preheat oven to 180C, 350F, GM4

Beat butter and sugar until soft

Add lemon zest, eggs and vanilla and cream together

Measure out flour

Spoon 4 tbsp flour into a bowl and add blueberries

Toss to ensure they are covered with flour

Set aside

Gradually spoon remaining flour and baking powder in to butter & sugar mix, alternating with splashes of milk

Gently fold in lemon juice, remaining flour and blueberries

Spoon into a greased pan, sprinkling with 1 tbsp sugar

Bake in oven for 35-40 minutes (or until a knife or skewer inserted near centre comes out clean)

Cooks Note: This cake freezes well.
If you don't have buttermilk, replace with milk, mix in 1 tbsp of lemon juice for every 175ml milk, and leave to stand for 20 minutes.

Banana Bread Tray Bake

This is full of flavour, chewy and delicious. It's also a great way of using up any overripe bananas.

Ingredients

Makes 24-30

250g butter
250g caster sugar
2 tbsp honey
5 eggs, beaten
450g self raising flour
2 tsp baking powder
½ tsp bicarbonate of soda
½tsp salt
3 ripe bananas, mashed
50g pecans, chopped
Milk, as required

Makes 12-15

125g butter
125g caster sugar
1 tbsp honey
3 eggs, beaten
225g self raising flour
1 tsp baking powder
1/4 tsp bicarbonate of soda
1/4 tsp salt
2 ripe bananas, mashed
25g pecans, chopped
Milk, as required

Preheat oven to 180C, 350F, GM4

Put the butter, sugar and honey in a bowl

Beat until light & fluffy

Add beaten eggs, a little at a time, mixing in with a spoonful of flour each time

Fold in the rest of the flour, baking powder, bicarbonate of soda and salt

Add bananas and pecans

Add enough milk to form a dropping consistency

Whisk until mixture is light and fluffy

Pour the mixture into a greased or lined baking tin

Bake in oven for 35-45 minutes

Leave to cool in tin

Cut into slices

Cooks Note: If you're out of pecans, try using raisins, sultanas, pine nuts or flaked almonds instead.

* Freezes well

Raspberry & Coconut Slice

Here's one for the coconut lovers - a three layer cake,
topped with coconut.

Ingredients

Serves 20-24

Cake

200g butter
220g caster sugar
4 eggs, beaten
300g flour
1 ½ tsp baking powder
300g raspberry jam

Topping

4 eggs
325g desiccated coconut
150g caster sugar

Serves 10-12

Cake

100g butter
110g caster sugar
2 eggs
185g flour
3/4 tsp baking powder
150g raspberry jam

Topping

2 eggs
160g desiccated coconut
75g caster sugar

Preheat oven to 350F, 180C, GM4

Grease baking tin

Cream together the butter and sugar, until soft

Add in egg, beating until mixture is light and smooth

Sieve flour and stir into mixture

Spread this paste evenly over baking pan using back of spoon

Spread raspberry jam evenly over this mixture

Mix eggs, coconut and sugar together

Spoon this mixture over the layer of jam and smoothly out evenly

Bake for 35 minutes

FUN FOR KIDS

Chocolate Toffee Slice

This is an easy no-bake favourite that you'll be asked to make again and again. Kids and adults love it!

Ingredients

Makes 20-24

5 Mars Bars (53g each) or 265g of Mars Bars
125g butter
120g crisped rice cereal, rice bubbles or snaps
200-230g milk chocolate
30g butter

Makes 10-12

2 ½ Mars Bars (53g each) or 130g of Mars Bars
65g butter
60g crisped rice cereal, rice bubbles or snaps
100-115g milk chocolate
15g butter

Chop and melt the Mars Bars and butter slowly in a pan

Pour in the Rice Krispies

Stir together until all the rice is coated

Pour into a greased slice tin or baking pan and press down gently

Melt milk chocolate and remaining butter in microwave

Pour melted chocolate over the top of the Rice Krispie mixture

Smooth across the top of the mix

Once cool, cut into slices

Chocolate Toffee Slice

Apricot Muesli Bar | Muesli Slice

This is an easy recipe that kids will love to cook or eat. It's a store cupboard favourite to produce healthy snacks for lunch boxes or teatime. It's half cake, half muesli bar, quite delicious, soft and tasty!

Ingredients

Makes 30 slices

300g butter
150g honey
225g sugar
150g self raising flour
200g oats
140g raisins or sultanas
150g chopped dates
375g chopped apricots
2 eggs, beaten
4 drops vanilla extract

Makes 15 slices

150g butter
75g honey
110g sugar
75g self raising flour
100g oats
75g raisins or sultanas
75g chopped dates
175g chopped apricots
1 egg, beaten
2 drops vanilla extract

Preheat oven to 180C, 350F, GM4

Melt butter & honey together

Add in sugar until dissolved

In a separate bowl, mix together remaining dry ingredients

Pour melted butter mix into dry ingredients

Add in egg & vanilla

Spoon in to a baking tin and press down

Bake for 20-25 minutes

Cool and slice to serve

Jelly Slice

This is a popular Australian recipe that deserves a wider audience. This tastes good, is loved by kids and adults. Its coloured layers are a colourful and fun treat for Christmas or kids parties!

Ingredients

Serves 12-16

Base Layer

200g Marie biscuits / Rich Tea biscuits (crushed)
175g butter (melted)

Middle Layer

3 tsp gelatine
75ml boiling water
405g tin condensed milk
2 lemons, juiced

Top Layer

1 pack red jelly (e.g. raspberry or strawberry)
550ml boiling water

Base Layer

Mix crushed biscuits and melted butter together

Press into base of well-greased or lined tin

Cool in fridge

Middle Layer

Dissolve gelatine in boiling water

Mix milk, lemon juice and gelatine mix

Pour on top of biscuits base and chill until set

Top Layer

Make jelly according to pack instructions

Pour onto top of chilled milk layer (whilst still in fridge to prevent spills, if possible!)

Chill until set

Cooks Note: for a slightly healthier option, replace middle layer with sliced bananas dipped in lemon juice

Bread Pudding Slice

This is a traditional tray bake that tastes delicious when hot or cold It's great for creatively using up stale bread.

Ingredients

Serves 24

500g stale bread (thick crust removed & torn or cut into 3cm square pieces)
500ml milk
4 eggs
8 tbsp milk
200g melted butter
300g sultanas or currants
150g soft brown sugar
2-3 tsp ground mixed spice
Sprinkle of ground or freshly grated nutmeg
2 tbsp granulated sugar

Serves 12

250g stale bread (torn or cut into pieces)
250ml milk
2 eggs
4 tbsp milk
100g melted butter
150g sultanas or currants
80g soft brown sugar (or granulated sugar)
1-2 tsp ground mixed spice (or to taste)
Sprinkle of ground or freshly grated nutmeg
1 tbsp granulated sugar

Preheat oven to 180C, 350F, GM4

Grease deep dish or tin with butter or line with foil

Soak bread pieces in milk and leave until well-soaked and soft

Mix eggs and spoonfuls of milk together, add in melted butter

In a bowl mix together dried fruit, sugar, mixed spice and soaked bread pieces

Add in egg, milk and butter mixture

With a large spoon, mix these together well

Spoon the mixture into the prepared dish

Sprinkle with freshly grated nutmeg and sugar (this helps create a crunchy topping)

Bake for 45-50 minutes or until golden

Cut into pieces and leave to cool

Cooks Note: Freeze stale bread until needed for this recipe.

If using fresh bread, slice and leave open to the air for 30 minutes - 2 hours, until bread feels dry to the touch.

GLUTEN FREE

Chocolate Brownie Tray Bake

Chocolate brownies with a hint of orange, this recipe is one of my favourites and it's freezer friendly too.

Ingredients

Serves 24-32

400g chopped milk chocolate
100g dark chocolate
500g butter
10 eggs (or 8 large eggs)
200g caster sugar
grated rind of two oranges
120g ground almonds (almond flour)
2 Tbsp cocoa
4 tsp instant coffee
6 tsp hot water

Serves 12-16

200g chopped milk chocolate
50g dark chocolate
250g butter
5 eggs (or 4 large eggs)
100g caster sugar
grated rind of an orange
60g ground almonds (almond flour)
1 tbsp cocoa
2 tsp instant coffee
3 tsp hot water

Preheat oven to 190C, 375F, GM5

Melt chocolates and butter together in a bowl over a pan of hot water (or microwave) until just melted

Set aside to cool for 5-10 minutes

Beat eggs together

Add sugar, grated orange rind to eggs and beat until well mixed and creamy

Add cooled chocolate and butter mixture

Finally add the ground almonds, cocoa, coffee powder and hot water

Pour the mix into a pan

Bake for 25 minutes

Cool brownies & cut into squares

Can freeze for up to 3 months

Cooks Note: Great served warm or cold with a generous spoonful of whipped cream or crème fraîche.

Gluten free recipe
** Freezer friendly

Flapjack Traybake Recipe

This is the recipe handed down to me by my mother. I fondly remember the wonderful smell of this baking and the pleasure of eating it warm from the oven.

Ingredients

Makes 36

500g butter
3 tbsp golden syrup
625g oats
350g sugar
1 ½ tsp ginger

Makes 24

285g butter
2 ½ tbsp golden syrup
425g oats
285g sugar
1 heaped tsp ginger

Makes 12

150g butter
1 ½ tbsp golden syrup
140g sugar
215g oats
½ tsp ginger

Preheat oven to 160C, 325F, GM3

Melt butter and golden syrup together in a saucepan, taking care not to boil

Stir in porridge oats, sugar and ginger & mix together

Spoon mixture into greased or lined tin

Bake in oven for 18-23 minutes, when it is light golden brown

A few minutes after removing from the oven, mark out slices

Leave to cool

* Gluten Free (if you use gluten-free oats)

All-in-One Chocolate Cake

This is an easy cake to make, just put together all the ingredients and voila! - a deliciously chocolatey and moist cake.

Ingredients

Serves 12

200g dark chocolate
200g cooked beetroot
300g ground almonds (almond flour)
75g cornflour
1 heaped tsp baking powder
1 dessert spoon cocoa
175g sugar
4 large or 5 medium eggs

Serves 24

400g dark chocolate
400g cooked beetroot
600g ground almonds (almond flour)
150g cornflour
2 heaped tsp baking powder
2 dessert spoon cocoa
350g sugar
8 large or 10 medium eggs

Preheat oven to 180C, 350F, GM4

Melt chocolate

Grate beetroot

Meanwhile, mix together almonds, cornflour, baking powder, cocoa, sugar, grated beetroot and eggs.

Finally, stir in chocolate, mixing well

Pour into a greased baking pan

Bake for 35-45 minutes

Cooks Note: Use the best dark chocolate, 70% or more, for the best results and for a dairy-free cake

* Gluten free
** Dairy free (use 70% dark chocolate and check the ingredients list to be sure)

Gluten Free Brownies Tray Bake

The indulgent mix of dark chocolate and almonds make these brownies inviting.

Ingredients

Serves 24

200g butter
200g caster sugar
150g dark chocolate (preferably 70% cocoa or more)
6 eggs
4 tsp vanilla extract
4 tbsp honey or 4 tbsp agave nectar
150g ground almonds
4 tsp baking powder
250g chopped walnuts

Serves 12

100g butter
100g caster sugar
75g dark chocolate (preferably 70% cocoa or more)
3 eggs
2 tsp vanilla extract
2 tbsp honey or 2 tbsp agave nectar
75g ground almonds
2 tsp baking powder
125g chopped walnuts

Preheat oven to at 180C, 350F, GM4

Grease a baking pan

Cream together butter and sugar

Melt the chocolate

Add eggs, vanilla and honey or agave nectar to the creamed butter and sugar mix

Stir in the melted chocolate

Mix in ground almonds, baking powder and nuts

Stir together until well mixed

Pour into baking pan

Bake for 25 minutes

Leave to cool before cutting into slices

Gluten free recipe

NO BAKE | NO COOK

Polish Cake | Chocolate Tiffin Slice

This was a childhood favourite that my mother used to make, the dates and the chocolate are a wonderful combination.

Ingredients

Serves 10-12

100g butter
1 tbsp golden syrup
250g biscuits (e.g. digestives or shortbread), crushed
75g chopped dates
2 dessert spoons drinking chocolate
150g chocolate

Serves 20-24

200g butter
2 tbsp golden syrup
500g biscuits (e.g. digestives or shortbread), crushed
150g chopped dates
4 dessert spoons drinking chocolate
300g chocolate

Melt the butter and golden syrup together in a saucepan

Add crushed biscuits, dates and drinking chocolate

Mix well and put into a baking tin

Melt chocolate, pour & spread over the top

Leave to cool

Cut into slices once cooled

Chocolate Tiffin

Hedgehog Slice

This is a great quick no-bake recipe which you can make from store cupboard ingredients.

Ingredients

Makes 24-35

200g shortbread fingers/Scotch Finger/TimTam biscuits or Rocky bars
275g dried fruit - eg sultanas or chopped dates
4-6 tbsp desiccated coconut (depending on preference)
2 tbsp cocoa
250g butter
300g milk chocolate
2 tsp vanilla extract

Makes 14-18

100g shortbread fingers/Scotch Finger/TimTam biscuits or Rocky bars
140g dried fruit - eg sultanas or chopped dates
2-3 tbsp desiccated coconut (depending on preference)
1 tbsp cocoa
125g butter
150g milk chocolate
1 tsp vanilla extract

Crush biscuits until size of crumbs, with a few chunks remaining

In a separate bowl, stir together dried fruit, coconut and cocoa

Melt butter and chocolate slowly

Stir melted butter, vanilla extract & chocolate into the broken biscuits

Stir together well

Spoon into a well-greased or lined baking tin and smooth down

Place in a cool place until set

When cool, cut into small, bite-size squares

Cooks Note: If you don't have shortbread fingers, try using whatever biscuits you have in the store cupboard.
Add 50g of chopped pecans for extra goodness.

Malty Indulgence Tray Bake

As the name suggests, this is rather indulgent, perfect for a special treat.

Ingredients

Serves 24-32

Base

200g butter
5 tbsp golden syrup
400g milk chocolate
410g Maltesers
400g digestive biscuits, crushed

Topping

400g milk chocolate
50g Maltesers (optional)

Serves 12-16

Base

100g butter
3 tbsp golden syrup
200g milk chocolate
200g Maltesers
200g digestive biscuits, crushed

Topping

200g milk chocolate
30g Maltesers (optional)

Melt together butter, golden syrup and chocolate

Cut Maltesers roughly in half

Pour in biscuits and Maltesers

Stir until well mixed

Spoon into a baking tin & smoothly out evenly

Melt remaining chocolate and pour over

Decorate with remaining Maltesers (optional)

Cut into pieces before fully cooled

Cooks Note: This can be frozen, so make ahead plenty of special treats.

BAKE TO IMPRESS

Ginger Butter Cake

A little different, if you enjoy shortbread and ginger, this is definitely one to try.

Ingredients

Serves 14-20

275g plain flour
Pinch of salt
200g caster sugar
200g butter - cut into pieces
75g stem ginger, cut into small pieces
1 large egg, beaten

Serves 28-40

550g plain flour
Pinch of salt
400g caster sugar
400 butter - cut into pieces
150g stem ginger, cut into small pieces
2 large eggs, beaten

Preheat oven to 350F, 180C, GM4

Mix flour and salt together

Add sugar and butter

Rub in butter

Add ginger and most of the egg

Mix to a dough like consistency

Smooth down into a baking tin

Brush with remaining egg

Bake for 35-40 minutes

Slice before it cools

Cooks Note: Tastes even better after 24 hours, as the ginger flavour deepens.

Lamington Bake

Inspired by Lamingtons, a traditionally Australian cake, a wonderful idea combining moist sponge, together with chocolate and coconut. Yummy!

Ingredients

Serves 24

Cake

250g butter
325g sugar
4 eggs
550g self raising flour
400ml milk
1 tsp vanilla extract

Topping

2 tbsp water
20g butter
80g icing sugar, sifted
2 tbsp cocoa, sifted
30g desiccated coconut

Serves 12

Cake

125g butter
165g sugar
2 eggs
275g self raising flour
200ml milk
½ tsp vanilla extract

Topping

1 tbsp water
10g butter
40g icing sugar, sifted
1 tbsp cocoa, sifted
15g desiccated coconut

Cake

Preheat oven to 180C, 350F, GM4

Cream butter and sugar until smooth

Beat eggs together

Add egg mix into butter mix a spoonful at a time

Mix in flour, salt, vanilla and milk

Mix until smooth

Pour into a baking tin

Bake for 25-30 minutes

Allow to cool

Topping

Melt water and butter together in a saucepan

Sift together sugar and cocoa

Add to water & butter

Stir until smooth

Thin with hot water, if needed

Pour icing on top of cake and smooth evenly

Sprinkle on desiccated coconut

Serve when icing is fully set

Lamington Bake

Chocolate Treacle Brownie Slice

If you just need something with a chocolate (or festive twist for Christmas), this is perfect. Of course, it's yummy to eat all year round too!

Ingredients

Serves 24-32

350g butter
2 tbsp black treacle (molasses)
400g dark chocolate
250g sugar
1 tsp vanilla extract
300g plain flour
Pinch of salt
6 eggs, beaten
100g chopped pecans

Serves 12-16

175g butter
1 tbsp black treacle (molasses)
200g dark chocolate, chopped or broken into pieces
125g sugar
½ tsp vanilla extract
150g plain flour
Pinch of salt
3 eggs, beaten
50g chopped pecans

Grease a baking pan

Over a low heat, melt butter, treacle and chocolate together

Stir in sugar, vanilla, flour and salt

Stir in beaten eggs and chopped nuts

Stir together

Pour into baking pan

Bake for 15-18 minutes

Cool and cut into slices

Carpathian Mountain Cake (Karpatka)

This is a Polish recipe which we first tasted in Polish food shops and loved so much that we hunted down the recipe.

The name comes from the look of the cake which resembles the snow-capped mountains of Carpathia.

Ingredients

Serves 12-18

Custard Filling

1 litre milk
225g sugar
5 tbsp flour
5 tbsp cornflour/cornstarch or potato starch
5 egg yolks
1tsp vanilla extract
175g butter

Choux Pastry Base & Topping

150g flour
1 tsp baking powder
1/4 tsp salt
250ml water
85g butter
5 eggs

Custard Filling

Heat 750ml milk and sugar in a saucepan

Meanwhile, place remaining milk, flour, corn/potato starch, egg yolks and vanilla in a bowl and mix until smooth

When milk mixture is hot enough for bubbles to form around the edge of the pan, take off heat and stir in the milk, flour and egg mixture

Return to a gentle heat stirring constantly until thickened

Cover, allow to cool, then beat in softened butter

Choux Pastry Base & Topping

Preheat oven to 200C, 400F, GM6

Mix flour, baking powder and salt together in a small bowl.

Heat water and butter together in a pan until boiling

Remove from heat and stir in flour mixture

Beat together until it forms into a ball, then set aside to cool

When lukewarm, add eggs one at a time, until mix is smooth and shiny

Spread mix between two well-greased or lined pans of equal size (9" square approx)

Bake for 25-30 minutes until golden, then set aside to cool

To assemble your Karpatka, remove a choux pastry from tin

Line the now empty tin with baking paper or foil

Replace the first pastry & spread filling over first pastry base

Top with the second pastry, with top side facing upwards

Chill in fridge for an hour or more

Serve dredged with icing sugar, slice with a sharp knife

Almond Frangipane

This is so easy to make, looks quite impressive and tastes delicious. This works well as a traybake, but for the best appearance, bake in a circular flan dish.

Ingredients

Serves 18-24

Pastry

400g plain flour
200g butter
100g caster sugar
2 eggs
Water

Filling

250g ground almonds *
250g softened butter
250g caster sugar
4 eggs
2 egg yolks
2 tbsp plain flour
50-100g berries

Serves 8-12

Pastry

200g plain flour
100g butter
50g caster sugar
1 egg
Water

Filling

125g ground almonds
125g softened butter
125g caster sugar
2 eggs
1 egg yolk
1 tbsp plain flour
Handful of berries

* Almond flour

Preheat oven to 180C, 350F, GM4

Grease or line a dish or tin

Mix together the flour, butter and sugar until the mixture resembles breadcrumbs

Add egg

Add cold water as required, until pastry comes together

Roll out and line dish or tin

Mix remaining ingredients, except berries, together in a bowl

Pour mix into the dish and spread evenly

Decorate with berries, pushing them gently into mix

Bake for 20-25 minutes, or until golden and slightly cracked appearance on top

Leave to cool, then cut into slices

Cooks Note: Use fresh or frozen berries, e.g. raspberries, blueberries, etc. Stoned cherries also work well with this recipe.

Almond Frangipane

About The Author

Elizabeth Daniel is a mother and a grandmother.

Elizabeth lives on the south coast of England, near the New Forest and Stonehenge.

She loves to bake for family and friends - whether it's every day or for a special occasion.

Printed in Great Britain
by Amazon

49594673R00061